Surf Sounds

Surf Sounds

Poems by

Roger Higgins

Liquid Light Press

Premium Chapbook First Edition

Copyright © 2014 by Roger Higgins

ISBN-10: 0990926702

ISBN-13: 978-0-9909267-0-2

Liquid Light Press

poetry that speaks to the heart

www.liquidlightpress.com

Cover Photo & Cover Design by M. D. Friedman
(*www.mdfriedman.com*)
Photo of Poet by Diana Higgins

Contents

Coquimbo

I walk in the direction of Coquimbo
towards the mighty cross
that dangles like a wish
above the workers' city
with its little windows looking down
on backyard gardens struggling in rock.
The blessing of a visiting Pope
has turned the plaza into a bazaar
of postcards and holy trinkets.

I skirt the edges of the spent waves
to protect my jeans and sneakers.

Some walks on the beach involve sun,
others rain, sometimes broken shells
or broken promises
and phosphorescent jellies
that reflect an inner pleasure.
A lone gull picks with a sharp beak
at a skeletal fish
like a critic at a raw nerve.

Suddenly I have soggy jeans
forgetting that one wave
like a thought
will be bigger than the rest.

How to take a shower

Wet your matted hair
shampoo out the tangles
in your brain

Rinse consternation
down the plughole with the suds

Pause a few moments
for conditioning
Let nutrients
soften your brittle mind

Save water and long-chain hydrocarbons
by washing also socks and jocks

Tackle armpits, crotch and memory pockets
with a scrub to these hidden places

Last, stand naked and with a rubber blade
scrape the inside spotless

La Sebastiana

The poet's prized binoculars
that spied on rooftop sunbathers
and made circular portraits of ships
restrain in their chambers
the arcing rockets
that painted the town red
each new year

This is a house
only a dreamer could love
so many slippery stairs
to be navigated
after all the wine
at all the parties
after the admiring guests
have headed off
or fallen asleep in a huddle

(Where are the photographs in the hall
of Neruda with a shoulder strapped
or a wrist in plaster?)

The sun floods the salons
the audio guide
cannot drown the carousing
that the walls remember

La Sebastiana looks down
towards the afternoon ocean
through unfocused eyes
briefly diverted from the incongruous
wooden horse
and the table set
waiting for eight guests
all gone
and a collector's zest
for pieces of anything

Beach at Mancora

An uninterrupted arc of glare-white sand
is exposed to the Pacific's wide fetch
but today the sea is unruffled

A clutch of riders sunbake on their boards
re-living point breaks and pipelines

The waves rise and fall
crest to trough
less than a bronzed torso

*

Blood-faced buzzards
scavenge at heads and tails
washed in on the tide
picking out eyes

In the backwash
plastic bags
slime my ankles

An outbreak of styrofoam trays
ulcerates the tide line

*

The membrane that divides
delight and disappointment
stretches, tears

the concomitant sludge
splashes, blisters
the unguarded cheek

Aromatherapy

Her hands writhe across my back like coils of a broad-bellied snake.
I relax facedown with my nose and mouth in a doughnut pillow.
On the floor is a platter of seashells
pink scallop, white mollusc, and black mussel
slightly off-centre as if Yuko's foot
has kicked it aside
as she stands at my head squeezing
and releasing
like a boa-constrictor.
Her slick hands stop discretely
just short of my buttocks.

There is background music of Peruvian pipes.
I sense Yuko's silent move around the table to massage my legs
rhythmically up then down the length of calves and thighs
stopping again at my buttocks
to leave a no-man's-land
between backrub and leg stroke.
The stroking becomes more hurried and urgent and ends
with a single finger touch to my big toe.

The process is repeated on my arms
the same lascivious rubbing
the same speeding up
the same promissory touch
this time to the end of my finger.
I have barely noticed the room's aromas
of clary sage, marjoram, ylang ylang and neroli.

Weekend

Peanut butter on a teaspoon, burnt chocolate on my fingertip
A verdant Sauvignon blanc from the Hills
Waves like mood music crashing, on a distant beach
Your buttocks silky under my fingertip
No pyjamas no nightgown, spooned after sex
At midnight, bedsheets rustling

Dry cakiness of your daybreak lips, smiling
A breakfast of seaspray and singed toast
Tongue, snaring nectarine juice errant on my chin
Lazy cappuccino dusted with bitter cocoa
Unsweetened certainty, loving
You hot from the shower, draped in a towel

* * *

An algorithm written in haste for the afternoon
on the exhausted freeway, stench and brake lights
Caught in a riptide of shoppers lamenting summer's close
The mark-downs are a racket, artificial sweeteners
Lining up at cheerless registers and parkade booths
Breaking out, saying never-again, knowing that we will

In a roadside café, the comfort of deep-fried wings
Cajun chicken and a giant lemonade
Calmed by sounds like surf surge from the CD
Your fingertips unknotting my neck and shoulders
Until, sheltering behind our own front door
A spoonful of peanut butter, a syrupy nectarine

Atacama, Going West

An imposter looming over near hills
silvery top above a threatening brow
blushes in the last light

as we push on through dusk
        no foreground
just a white line reaching out
to the cordillera's silhouette
against a flat orange sky.

The lights of an approaching truck
are pinholes in this diorama.

We talk in broken silences
        time suspended
comfortably alone.

Our road climbs the mountains
and breaks through a high pass.

We descend into dark
just whitecaps in the headlight beams
the horizon retreating.

Last Night at the Moroccan Bar on Front Street

In the middle of my belly is a small round
deeply indented
vortexed cavity

Last night at the Moroccan bar on Front Street
a matching wound gazed back at me
I declare I saw it wink

as I watched the shimmying flesh
of loosely bound breasts and mounded
belly of the veiled dancer

Small bells jingled a sonata of fecundity
allure and expectation
around her undulating hips

Cumin and coriander
floated above braised lamb
and spiced coffee seared my throat

My belly-eye does not promise a whirlpool
tumble into the womb
I have there only a sack

filled with lamb and black coffee
behind the small round scar
in the middle of my belly

Cold Storage

From a middle rack I heard
the laughter of oranges
saw the shy intimacy of strawberries
and glimpsed a discreet
copulation of honeydews
challenging the priggishness of pineapples.

I found a sea breeze
as fresh and confident
as garden lettuce
wafting in the crisper
and wave-washed sandcastles
squatting like Christmas puddings.

The freezer was jam-packed
with a stock of memories
(better discarded)
of get-togethers
where friendships faltered
and lonely breakfasts taken
standing at the kitchen sink.

And in the icemaker tumbled cubes
of divergence and dissent
congealed
into a menacing mass
as chilling
as an unspoken diagnosis.

What should I do
with a fridge like that?

Walking with Bears

This morning's scat scattered by wasps
broken branches on the berry bushes

flattened grass paths to the river bank
paw and claw impressions in the sand

for two days we have been walking with bears
but have not seen them; we know they have seen us

Fear is a simple human need like love is
but not like love, after all

who wants to overcome love?
We foster our fears

Suddenly ahead on a log sloping to the water
a grizzly mother with two new-season cubs

we tense and stare
she turns and guides her children away
into the forest

Which brings me around to pride
not one of the deadly sins, after all

but an expression of love
and our capacity to overcome fear

to look at what we have done and say
It is very good

Our parents fade from us and even from our memories
our children take children's risks

we wait for a diagnosis, or fishtail on black ice
and we know we are walking with bears

The Day the Beach Was Washed Away

I stood on a scarp where a gentle dune had stood
and estimated depth of erosion in metres
and width of the beach in tens of metres
and length of the beach in kilometres
and calculated tonnes of sand
swept out

and the number was a number – nothing more
there are more suns in the universe
than the grains of sand in all those tonnes
what I want to know is
when can I surf here again?
surging forward on a clean break without choppy backwash
the beach is in recession and I wonder who wins
maybe I'll just watch the waves rebuild
the beach

Killer Wind

It stings
like a cutting remark from a smiling face
causing me to withdraw
seek safe haven
in a knitted cap and leather gloves
zip my windbreaker high against my chin
turn and be pushed away
down the beach

The killer wind
is icy
it mocks the clear sky and a sun that can warm
only through glass

I walk away only so far before I must turn
back into the face of it
slicing the sand into wafers and stringers

Caught between the monster and the whirlpool
getting away or coming back
I can grit my teeth
or grin

Gritting and grinning use different muscles
require different strengths
and next morning
hurt in different places

I scrutinize the smiling sky
rug up against the cutting wind
take cover
behind a transparent shield

Labour Day

On Labour Day we try to do as little work as possible
sprawled on someone's sleeping legs
reading Robert Wrigley's recent slender volume
learning new words for fears of many and specific kinds.

One of the Williams sisters makes the round of sixteen
our home teams win at baseball and lose badly at football
or perhaps it is the other way around it is so hard to tell
with so much sun in our eyes and hockey on the horizon.

We barely flinch at blockbuster gore and body count
but worry that the younger ones will get wrong ideas
should they glimpse a nipple or a buttock fondly stroked.

We worry about taxes that we can afford to pay
substitute chants and rants for wisdom and ideas
and this is how the summer ends, as dreams turn cold.

Sharp Edges

today the world has sharp edges
which tear at the sleeves of my jacket

the sky is falling
or at least the markets are
which is pretty much the same thing
these days

the carpet is warm lard
the room smells yellow
the coffee sulphurous

even the fastidious straight-backed chair
winces beneath me
in sympathy

I wish I had stayed in bed
but I had lain too long
on the soft white pillow
of insomnia

what feels good
is that I can pee
all the way to Wall Street
through a hole in the world
the size of a latrine

Flotsam

Just north of Copiapó is a ridge
like the spine of a salt-water croc
with outcrop eyes and cosine tail.
The next has small sand dunes
like scales on a snapper;
then row on row of sharp-backed crests
like a school of tunafish.

In this Cretaceous ocean
I am swept like seaweed against rocks
and dragged like an anchor over sandy bottoms;
struggle to stand, struggle to breath
feel lightheaded with lead-weight boots.
The gluttonous depths of the desert
swallow me whole then spew me out
through a chasm,
like a discarded plank
on the welcome shore
of the Pacific.

Dunes

Small dunes scallop up the beach
retreating from the cold wind
They try to ripple across the highway
but the smooth black asphalt defeats them
slicing them into wafers just a few grains thick
which dissipate on the stony plain

A sand grain diaspora
massing across the frontier of water's edge
clustering mixing
contaminating and being contaminated
diluting and being diluted
energizing and being energized
a part and apart
their sand-grain DNA
always traceable
always remembering
the mother land

Lament to the Sound of Waves

Surf surge
I strain to hear
the ocean beat against the desert.
I wonder for a moment
at the geographic oddity
of Africa, the Atacama and Australia
and their arid western fringes.

She sits on a rock at Playa Amarillo,
she tells me through static,
a million miles from where we were together.
I listen behind the nervous chatter
from her cell phone,
filtering ethereal surf sounds
interfering with the real thing

willing memories of the good times
on the rocks and in the rock pools
with anemones and soldier crabs
and broken shell beaches
like broken dreams

remember only the good times

watching the sun dissolve in the Pacific
turning the ocean orange,
laughing uncontrollably
as we are stranded by a rising tide
of indifference

shaking the salty water from canvas shoes
and crunching the broken shell dreams
as we turn
to face the naked hills,
where four-track trails
lead over impasses to desolate valleys

only the good times

the sea a royal-rich blue
the desert khaki-cold
the line between so sharp
it could cut out your heart.
The good times,
enough I hope
to last a lifetime alone,
except for surf surge
mixed with static.

The Mother

She made her way along the rocky shoreline
turning over rocks
searching for crabs and small fish
stranded by the tide.

She has three cubs
our guide said in low voice
Look in the tall tree
back from the beach.

Soon the mother left the rocks for the forest
and emerged with three
trailing apostrophes
that tumbled behind her
to the water's edge.
We nudged closer in the boat.

They ignored us until
we don't know how or why
the mother sent the cubs scurrying
back to the cover of the trees
while she continued
to search under rocks.

Close behind
a raven checked each overturned rock
for molluscs.

Living Underwater during Drought

each tramcar platform in King William Street
is besieged by school kids
tropical fish in school colors
that swim and swarm
below the waveform dip and rise
of wires and cables that distort the sky

the brightly painted trams
are nudibranchs that creep and pause
creep and pause from reef to reef
until at Glenelg their tentacles sense
seagrasses and leafy dragons
so they pause and creep away

backlit clouds smudge the horizon
we are in a hot haze between sea and sky
between wet and dry
we struggle for breath with tight lips
while in flared nostrils
the smell of rain would be heaven sent

Long Poem

There is a place for the long poem,
for the long night
turning fitfully between damp sheets
in a lonely bed
There is a place for the long shoreline
empty except for me
and your likeness in a cloud

There is a place for the long life
with these coordinates —
my mother, my father, you
a child and then another
a grandchild

And how was I supposed to know until now
that you would still be my lover and friend
now that we have spent most of our lives
together?
How intriguing to have
this sudden knowing
after these decades, our children full-grown.

There is a place in our life for the long death,
for the long silence
and a surf on the long shoreline
under the edge of the sky

The Flat Roof of the Shed

As a boy he would lie on his back
spread-eagled over the corrugated iron
on the flat roof of the shed.
He would look for familiar faces in the clouds,
his second grade teacher as she tried and failed
and tried again to make him a right-hander
leaning over his shoulder to gently take the pencil
from one hand and place it in the other,
and the long unshaven face of his grandfather
who kept a high gloss on the old green chevy
and sometimes let him ride in the rumble seat.
The boy would anticipate whether the next arrow head
would drag a contrail in from the north or south
turning the sky on a clear day
into an ancients' map of the world with places
that were just names to him around the rim
and himself in the centre.
He did not feel the metal ridges
under his shoulder blades and buttocks
and easily filled in those aimless hours
between school and the family dinner
climbing down at the last minute to do his chores
bringing in wood for the combustion stove
or picking fresh corn and carrots from the garden.

This Mostly Moribund Self

Today, my tasks are few and palm
leaves are providing my cover
as peddlers skirt around indulgent hotel staff
forbidding their incursions to the pool deck.
Our light shorts and tops
are the livery of beach goers everywhere
getting this respite from northern sub-zeros.
Impossible to stop eyes or nose
or mouth, tropical senses alert to stimuli
each disparate, each distinction
clear, our separation
from here to home complete.
Let your world news replay
on unwatched screens
commotion crowded-out by unconcern
that we are missing anything
in our sabbatical revelry and
debris-dissipating timeout.
This mostly moribund self,
I swear half-heartedly,
isn't going to be taunted into thinking.

About the Author

Roger Higgins has been published in various magazines and journals. His collection, *Hieroglyphs*, appeared in *New Poets 13* (Friendly Street Poets). He is an Australian who has travelled widely and lived in (alphabetically) Canada, Chile, Papua New Guinea, Scotland, and the USA. Roger is an engineer by vocation, and has utilized his pen rather more than his camera on many of his travels, bringing together his physical and emotional responses to the environments and situations which he has encountered. First versions may be written on paper napkins or pieces of paper tablecloths, the backs of boarding passes or the notes screen of a mobile phone.

Acknowledgements and Credits

I would like to recognize the encouragement and advice of my family and friends, Friendly Street Poets, Juliet Patterson and the Poetry Exchange group facilitated by Alice Osborn. The following poems first appeared in the publication listed after each in parenthesis:

"Flotsam" & "How to walk on the beach" (*Hieroglyphs - New Poets 13*),

"Lament to the Sound of Waves" (*Tamba*),

"Atacama, Going West" (*Readers' World*),

"The Day the Beach Was Washed Away" (*Mindscape*), and

"Labour Day" (*Friendly Street Poets 38*).

Other Books from Liquid Light Press

All Liquid Light Press books are available directly from *liquidlightpress.com* or from any of the current major global distribution channels including Amazon, Barnes and Noble, the iBookstore and the Ingram Catalog.

***Leaning Toward Whole*, Poems by M. D. Friedman (Released June, 2011)**
This poetry chapbook from the international award winning poet, M. D. Friedman, contains pieces both poignant and personal.

***The Miracle Already Happening – Everyday Life with Rumi*, Poems by Rosemerry Wahtola Trommer (Released December, 2011)**
Rosemerry Wahtola Trommer's superb collection of poems, inspired by Rumi, is full of heart, humor, peace and wisdom.

***Spiral*, Poems by Lynda La Rocca (Released March, 2012)**
Award winning poet, Lynda La Rocca, creates a compelling poetic and melodic discourse from the persistent cravings and fears inside of each of us.

***From the Ashes*, Poems by Wayne A. Gilbert (Released June , 2012)**
From the Ashes is a true masterpiece that gnaws at the heart with universal appeal.

***ah*, Poems by Rachel Kellum (Released July, 2012)**
Rachel Kellum's poetry has a simplicity and clarity that cuts to the core of being human.

***Catalyst*, Poems by Jeremy Martin (Released December, 2012)**
Catalyst may just launch you on the fiery ride into yourself.

***Of Eyes and Iris*, Poems by Erika Moss Gordon (Released March, 2013)**
Beautiful yet poignant in its simplicity, *Of Eyes and Iris*, will call you back again and again for another read.

***Your House Is Floating*, Poems by Susan Whitmore (Released June, 2013)**
Susan Whitmore's craft is as smooth, crisp and satisfying as olive oil on fresh garden greens.

***Nowhere Near Morning*, Poems by Jeffrey M. Bernstein (Released October, 2013)**
Nowhere Near Morning is an intimate embrace of what it means to be alive, a wakeup call for those falling asleep at the wheel of their daily grind.

***Harmonica*, Poems by Cecele Allen Kraus (Released March, 2014)**
Harmonica bristles with a shimmering music that heals the heart.